# BUD'S BOOK

*of*

# POETRY

# BUD PEKA

ISBN 979-8-88832-736-4 (paperback)
ISBN 979-8-88832-737-1 (digital)



Christian Faith Publishing
832 Park Avenue
Meadville, PA 16335
www.christianfaithpublishing.com

Printed in the United States of America

OWATONNA

# Contents

# Good Friday

I envision the cross on which Christ died,
on the day that He was crucified,
He gave up His life for you and for me,
thus, began our Christianity.

As we recall Christ's death today,
let us bow down our heads and pray,
That we live our lives in spirituality,
so we might join Him in eternity.

# Fingers by God

When you pick up a hair or a string,
or some other minute thing,
observe the dexterity
of your fingers,
a gift from God.

Man has made no machine,
that can compare,
with a thumb and a finger,
for picking up hair.

Can a machine pick your nose,
flick a booger,
or pull up ladies' hose?

What but a thumb,
can thumb a ride?

What can pull down your eyelid,
to put drops in your eyes?
What but a finger,
can point to a plane in the sky?

Pointing upward with the middle finger,
is an insulting form of salutation,
which is now quite commonplace,
in our great nation.

So as you go about your daily chores,
be always aware of the danger that lingers,
to these tools which are only yours,
those precious, God-given fingers.

# Forever Friend

Old friends you have treasured,
for a long, long time,
are valuable indeed,
they are there for you,
and you for them,
in any hour or need.

You tell your troubles to them
likewise, they to you,
the best advice is given,
that is what we do,
consolation is a loving virtue.

When this friend is called away,
to answer the call of the Father,
for that loss, we can only pray.
God will also love His son or daughter,
and we pray that He will send,
another trusting, loving, forever friend.

# Fast Life

Let us not dwell on yesterday,
nor worry about tomorrow,
let's all enjoy the here and now,
time is something we can't borrow.

"He is living on borrowed time,"
what does that statement mean?
This poor soul is losing the fight,
his imminent demise is foreseen.

This is the day the Lord has made,
let us rejoice in it and be glad,
today we live at such a fast pace,
we miss His blessings, that is sad.

# Enter His Kingdom

If you have lost your faith in God,
and think you can live life on your own,
you'll soon learn that you're living all alone,
that your new belief system is quite flawed.

Perhaps you had a loving wife and family,
relatives, and oh-so-many, many friends,
but as your empty life now nears its end,
you'll realize the need for true spirituality.

Perhaps your lack of faith is getting scary,
so when you are out for a morning walk today,
why not step into the house of God to pray,
ask God to remove that sinful pride you carry.

Confess to Him those burdensome offenses,
kneel in humble prayer and supplication,
praise and honor the Lord in humble adoration,
ask that He bring you back to your good senses.

Nothing is more gratifying to those you leave behind,
than to know that even in the eleventh hour,
God's love and comfort and almighty power,
has given to them real peace of mind.

The deceased has found the love and comfort,
of God who welcomed this soul into His home,
eternal peace and happiness, they'll never feel alone,
that loving soul has been triumphant.

"The last shall be first and the first, last"
(The laborers in the fields, Matt. 20:1–16)

# Do Not Give Up on Life

Do you have thoughts of gloom and doom,
do you feel all alone in a crowded room,
perhaps you need a very special friend,
who'll be with you always, to the very end.
Just ask, it's all you need to do,
then Jesus will respond to you.
He'll help you in your hour of need,
He's there for you, that's guaranteed.
He'll be certain that you receive His love,
with His spiritual guidance from above.
My friend, if you are hurting deep inside,
plagued with thoughts of suicide,
this new friend has so much love to give,
He'll show you have so much life to live,
please, my friend, call out to Jesus,
to enter into your troubled life.
He'll remove those pains of sorrow and strife,
do it now, please don't delay,
drop down to your knees and pray.
I believe that as you pray and kneel,
He will hear your prayers,
then your mind will heal.

# Bridge to Eternal Happiness

On a resplendent, golden bridge,
I walked over the River of Peace.
It took me a lifetime to get there,
it was then that my life did cease.

T'was a long and arduous sojourn,
from my beginning until my end.
For this person, whom few folks knew,
I'm gone and will not return again.

I felt at peace down deep inside,
I had confessed my bad behavior.
I accepted Jesus Christ the Lord,
as my loving, personal Savior.

# CROSS OF ASHES

They will know that I am Christian,
by the cross of ashes on my head,
I will always remain a Christian,
until the day that I am dead.

I was baptized when just an infant,
I've been a Christian since that day,
when confirmed, I made a commitment,
I took Jesus as my Savior, and to Him, I pray.

I have tried to live a good life,
I hope and pray God welcomes me,
where there is no sorrow and strife,
from life's burdens, He will set me free.

# Calvary

Happy Easter, Christ is risen,
now our sins can be forgiven.
He gave up His life for our redemption,
His role, since Virgin Mary's conception.

He truly is the Son of God,
the Pharisees claimed He was a fraud.
Millions of Christians from many nations,
pray to Him and give humble adoration.

"Father, forgive them, for they know not what they do."
Remember, He died for me, He died for you.
His last words before He died, "It is finished."
Let our love for Jesus remain undiminished.
Jesus is my personal Savior.
Please join me.

# Bring Us Love and Peace

There is so much hatred in this world today,
please tell me, Jesus, has it always been this way?
That's a ridiculous question, I ask of you,
considering the atrocious death, they put you through.

Why can't we all live in peace together,
is it because some people think they're better?
Some folks hate others for the color of their skin,
that seems to me a scant reason, God, isn't that a sin?

How can so many millions in our nation go on living,
their daily lives, yet remain so very unforgiving?
There are so many who lay blame on our nation,
while their impoverished lives are their own creation.

For their inadequate education, they berate their schools,
which are turning out thousands of uneducated fools.
They did not study, many beat and injured teachers,
these students are looked upon as low-life creatures.

Lord, what is your solution to all of this mental pollution,
is all of this a prediction of a coming revolution?
You tell us that we must turn back to the preaching,
of your Son, Jesus, with His biblical teaching,
of justice, morality, and service to others,
let all people be like our sisters and brothers.

# We All Sail Our Own Boat

I am sailing in a tiny boat, that's afloat,
on that unpredictable ocean of life,
the winds of fate fill the sails of my boat,
I rejoice when everything seems just right.

At times, only a tranquil calm remains,
following the sea's wild, tempestuous roar,
but I long ago had discovered my lighthouse,
Jesus steers me clear of perilous, rocky shores.

He always knows what is best for me,
providing personal calmness, so I have no fear,
I constantly try to follow His moral compass,
He has charted a course for me to steer.

I try to live my life for Him, each and every day,
with a firm hand, I hold my boat on a steady course,
but at times, I have drifted from my chosen way,
after which I've suffered deep remorse.

From my launching, rough seas, now my salvation,
I have tried to follow in His footsteps while yet alive,
but now, my cruise is over, I'm at my destination,
I pray He'll welcome me into His house when I arrive.

# WORKS OF MERCY

You will leave your footprints,
in the sands of time, each day,
from the day that you are born,
until the day you'll pass away.

Your footprints tell so much about you,
how kind you've been to others,
to your siblings, dads, and mothers,
friends, enemies, and many others.

Help the troubled find their way,
teach them how and why to pray,
feed them when they're hungry,
give them a drink if they are thirsty.

Shelter those lonely homeless,
they must feel such aloneness,
offer clothes to keep them warm,
help protect them from street harm.

Give money so they are fed,
visit the sick and bury the dead,
visit the troubled prisoner,
always be a good listener.

Pray for those who've lost their lives,
those who have died by suicide,
nothing could ease their troubled minds,
pray for the family and friends they left behind.

# Wayward Young

Many lose the Lord when they are young.
Their young lives had just begun.
They live their lives in wicked sin.
They let that devil, Satan, win.

We pray, someday, they'll see the light,
—of Christ—
He will show them a new life, that's right.
Upon their knees, they'll listen to Him.
Then to God, will confess their sins.

They're now forgiven for things they had done.
Their great victory over sin is won.
Now they offer prayers to God each day
And find total happiness this way.

# THE LACK OF FAITH

The major cause of unhappiness,
in the world today,
I believe, is caused by the lack of faith,
and people's refusal to pray.

If we believed in a loving, living God,
and that He is always near,
there would be much more friendliness,
and much less personal fear.

There would be no ruthless rulers,
wanting to dominate the world,
there would be no war-torn nations,
with innocent people getting killed.

In the war against the powers of darkness,
prayer is the primary, mightiest weapon,
in the deliverance of these men from their power,
prayer and faith will help stop their evil aggression.

Let us pray for the innocent lives being taken,
in Putin's war on his neighbor, Ukraine.
All of the slaughter is a human tragedy,
on the people, he has inflicted too much pain.

# That Heavenly Port

It is much more difficult navigating,
up the River of Golden Dreams,
than floating toward your damnation,
down your own disinterested stream.

At the end of the River of Golden Dreams,
awaits a marvelous, shining Golden Gate.
I am quite certain you know that it means,
you've arrived here because of your faith.

Faith in the Father, faith in the Son,
you carried that faith all through your life.
Your battle to earn this invitation is won,
now just forget all past sorrows and strife.

That Heavenly Gate has now swung open,
you are invited to enter His kingdom,
by everyone, a common language is spoken,
forever in eternity, thy kingdom has now come.

# THE BRIDGE BUILDER

We need someone to build a bridge,
across our nation's great divide,
one to carry a message of love and peace,
to those on the other side.

Someone who can show all of us the way,
to respect one another's point of view,
please, dear Lord, let it happen today,
that's something we must all pursue.

Who is the one who can lead us, you ask,
I think we both know the answer, my friend.
He is the One who was crucified on the cross,
on His teachings, we can always depend.

He showed us the way to show love for one another,
how to live a life filled with goodness and love,
love of neighbor and honor of father and mother,
let us pray to Jesus, who is looking down from above.

# SHE STILL LIVES

I met an elderly man today,
sitting in the shade,
on a park bench, all alone,
I decided I would talk to him,
indeed, he seemed quite dismayed.

I sat down next to him, then asked,
"May I help you, my good man?"
He looked up at me with teary eyes,
"My wife died last week,
I know it was God's plan."

We sat here while on our daily walks,
on this very same bench, we sat,
we would stay here until well rested,
my, how she loved to sit and chat.

We'd watch the families as they played,
and young lovers strolling by,
happiness was all around us,
today, I only sit right here and cry.

Suddenly, he stopped crying, then he smiled,
"I just recalled the words of Jesus from John 11,
my darling wife and life companion,
is now living with Jesus in heaven."

"I know someday we'll be reunited again,
I don't know how, where, or when.
I miss her every minute of every day,
for the rest of my life, it will be this way.

I pray that the passage of time will heal,
my aching heart and the loss that I feel.
She was my life's companion and lover,
our children would often say,
"She was a wonderful, loving mother."

In John 11:25–26, Jesus said, "I am the resurrection and the life. The one who believes in me will live, even though they die; and whoever lives by believing in me will never die."

# I Am a Homeless Veteran

I'm a veteran of that long Mideast war,
I have seen way too much blood and gore,
I watched my buddies die near me,
They had accidentally stepped on an IED.

I also had stepped on an IED,
It shattered my leg up to the knee,
For six long months, I was in a cast,
I am very lucky I survived that blast.

Now I'm living in a homeless camp,
In San Diego, with druggies and tramps,
Many violent homeless live in this park,
It is extremely dangerous here after dark.

I suffer from post-traumatic stress disorder syndrome.
This homeless camp has become my home,
I have had thoughts that tell me to end my life,
After all I have lived through in sorrow and strife.

When I drifted off to sleep, last night,
There was a sudden, radiant beam of light,
Then I saw a vision of this young bearded man,
I could see huge, ugly scars on his hands.

He spoke with a soft and loving voice,
"In battle into danger, you had no choice,
I know you have seen some terrible sights,
That is why I'm here with you tonight."

"I know that you have been trying to decide,
Whether you should end your life by suicide,
I will not let that happen to you, my brother,
Just as I have also saved so many others."

"I am asking that you have total faith in me,
Let us pray now that to this you will agree,
I will lead you on a straight path in your life,
You will no longer suffer from internal strife."

I sprang up quickly, so wide awake was I,
His soothing words had made me cry,
The face and pierced hands that I had seen,
Have now vanished from my serene dream.

I knelt down, then bowed my head to pray,
I walked out of the homeless camp that day,
No longer do I think of not wanting to live,
I'll help other veterans, I have much love to give.

"Fear not, for I am with you; be not dismayed,
for I am your God; I will strengthen you,
I will help you, I will uphold you
with my righteous right hand."

For assistance, visit www.suicidepreventionlifeline.org
or the mental health crisis hotline at 988.

# Are You There? Do You Care?

As I lay here in my darkened room,
I pray for this world which is filled,
with sinful doom and gloom,
from their TVs, sports, and games,
many people won't turn away,
to see what is really happening,
in our wonderful nation today.

I am quite concerned about the future,
of our precious little kids,
they'll live in a once great power,
that literally has gone down the skids.

The devil's banner has been unfurled,
upon our deeply troubled world,
why, I ask you, my dear Lord,
is our nation spending our little wealth,
on so many things we can't afford.

Trillions here and trillions there,
they are throwing money everywhere,
which will burden future generations,
who will live in this once great nation.

It is time for us to return to God,
right now, to many, that sounds odd,
hopefully, they will learn what's right,
and will then follow His guiding light.

# Are You Prepared?

The clock of life keeps ticking on,
there'll come a day when your life is gone,
I go to church, and what do I see,
middle-aged and old folks just like me.

They come to the house of God to pray,
many come here almost every day.
Where are the young ones, don't they care?
When was the last time they said a prayer?

Do they not see that they, too, will die?
Their many loved ones will then cry.
Where will they go, to heaven or hell?
On those thoughts, they do not dwell.

Please, dear children, prepare to go,
where, when, and how, we just don't know.
Please, love the Lord, and in Him believe,
I pray you will find Him, before you leave.

# Mental Wilderness

Are you lost in the wilderness,
dissatisfied with your life,
blaming all of your troubles,
on your husband or your wife?

On your partner in your business,
perhaps you hate your daily work,
you just feel so very hopeless,
everyone you met today is just a jerk.

My friend, heed the words of Apostle Paul,
he said, "Cast your burdens upon the Lord,"
but some burdens, you alone must carry,
entry into heaven could be your reward.

You must give an account of the life you lived,
all of the days that you walked this journey,
those days when you were aggrieved,
and the days that in Christ, you believed,
do this before you're laid out on that gurney.

# AN ABSENT FATHER

He left his family homeless,
yet he calls himself a man.
They felt a terrible aloneness,
he just left them, then he ran.

He sends no money for either food or shoes,
his earnings are spent on drugs and booze.
Someday, he'll be a very lonely guy,
he'll have a small funeral, should he die.

He might live to a very old age,
but they'll forgive him, they show no rage.
They'll come to visit him now and then,
and have promised to be there at his end.

Let's believe God's Word, they tell each other,
we must honor our father and our mother.
Forgiveness is a virtue we must not ignore,
let's forgive this man, who left us so poor.

# Acknowledge Him

Hope and love from God above,
Love beyond our understanding,
He shows us the way every day,
His love is not demanding.

When you awaken in the morning,
Thank Him for another day,
Love your God and your neighbor,
Praise God as you go about your labor,
Let that always be your way.

# A Young Girl's Lament

When we were back in high school,
you taught me how to use,
I thought you were so very cool,
then you shared a joint with me,
and furnished me with booze.

Now looking back at that,
I now realize I had much to lose,
I see that I was just a fool,
'cause all you ever wanted,
were sex and drugs and booze.

Now you have left me with your baby,
for five years, while you're sitting in a cell,
I'll work to support your baby and think of you,
recalling the last words that you spoke to me were,
"You, bitch, just go to hell."

I just wanted to always love you,
I dreamed of being your loving bride,
I wanted to have a little home for two,
and some lovely smiling children,
we're all standing at your side.

My hard days and lonely nights make me very sad,
you have never written, no text, nor email do I get,
although I often write and send photos of your son,
with you, it's just like we have never met,
I will not be waiting until your prison time is done.

So long to you, my fantasy man of long ago,
I hope you will have, someday, a happy life,
I will raise our son to be a loving, caring man,
who will not ruin the lives of others,
a man who will love his children and his wife.

# A RIGHT TO LIFE

"How long is a life?" I asked my father,
"Why is it you worry, my son,
some folks live past one hundred,
then they're returned to the earth,
millions of babies die before birth."

"Why do some babies die before birth, sir,
and never see the light of day?"
"There is this thing called abortion,
it just takes their innocent lives away,
that's all that I will tell you today."

I go through my young life now wondering,
why is this done to those small precious ones,
father responded, "My son, I do not know."
It's the Supreme Court's law that they made,
it's due to the passage of Roe v. Wade.

A nurse, Margaret Sanger, and Sister Edith Byrne,
opened the first birth control clinic,
in Brooklyn, New York, back in 1916.
Planned parenthood soon arose from that scheme,
the Supreme Court Judge Blackmun, passed Roe v. Wade,
for forty-eight years, it has been the law of the land,
permitting abortions in the first three months of pregnancy,
and now some states allow it right up until birth,
or can take the life of a newborn child,
which just came out of the womb.

"That's the story as I understand it, my son,
remember these words when you're dating,
love and respect the girl and her chastity,
let there be no sex nor impregnating,
for that would be a most terrible tragedy."

"Now go live your life, be the best you can be,
you will never then, have to apologize to me,
nor to her parents, but especially to this lady,
and you need not worry about fathering an
unwanted baby."

# A Psalm of Supplication

The Holy Spirit has found me,
I feel His love surround me,
it warms my heart and soul,
total serenity is my goal,
this solace is so very comforting,
emanating from God, my King.
For one who has been so troubled,
at times I have really struggled,
with often needless worry,
for my sins, I've been so sorry.
When I now feel most helpless,
I pray fervently to Him to help us,
in my hour of greatest need,
Lord, from worries, let me be freed.
When I am weak, then I am strong,
help me to know right from wrong,
let my life resound like a happy song,
a song I will sing in prayer to you,
a quite proper thing to do,
for guidance in the early morning,
I rise to witness this day's dawning.

Please come, Holy Spirit, be with me,
lead me safely on my way, I implore thee,
Holy Spirit, God the Father, and the Son,
the Holy Trinity, we all know as One.
I have shouldered a heavy load,
as I have trudged along life's road,
You have blessed me on my way,
Without Your guidance, I'd not be here today.
Lord, now I ask in fervent prayer,
please embrace me with Your loving care.
I believe the Holy Spirit has found me,

feeling that Love astounds me,
it gives me peaceful rest each night,
my day is done, my Lord, goodnight.
*Amen*!

# A Mother's Prayers

My mother feared lightning storms at night. She woke me from my childhood sleep and took me into the kitchen to pray during the storm. Her prayers were heard; we were never struck by lightning. She died at ninety-five. I am ninety-five and have survived storms on land and sea. In the navy, in WWII, I encountered typhoons, submarine alerts, Japanese Kamikaze attacks, and shelling from cannons on shore. God is still hearing my mother's prayers for my safety. I haven't been struck by lightning. Yet. Thanks, Mother! RIP.

# A Loving Father

It takes a real man to be a good father,
who will raise a fine son and loving daughter,
with direction and love from his wonderful wife,
a loving family together makes a wonderful life.

As the head of the house, he is always there,
to help carry those burdens that they both share,
to raise their children in love and respect,
prepared for life, knowing what to expect.

Too many males carelessly plant their seed,
then abandon the mother in her hour of need,
then they will move on to discover another,
one more child, abandoned, with a single mother.

This scene is replayed all across our land,
none of the results had been wanted or planned,
too many of these unsuspecting young ladies,
who will become mothers to unwanted babies.

# It Is Your Country

America, America,
my heart bleeds for thee,
we have fought great wars,
and won those wars,
to keep our nation free.

Now we are a troubled land,
there's much civil unrest,
Marxists long have planned,
to take command,
they want to rule our land.

America, America,
we'll fight and win this war,
we're against their plan,
we do love this land,
America, free for evermore.

We will fight for the red,
white and blue,
and our Constitution too,
we will also fight,
to defend our bill of rights,
this is something we must do.

Let us return to God,
for His guidance from on high,
please don't abandon Him,
we can't give in to sin,
we must pray to Him,
or we'll watch our nation die.

America, America,
flag of red, white, and blue,
let's salute our flag,
and defend and love our flag,
the patriotic thing to do.

# I IMAGINE

I'm standing in death's valley,
gazing at that Golden House upon the hill.
It stands behind a Golden Wall, with Golden Gate,
I see a sign above that gate that reads,
Only the worthy may enter here,
all others please use the iron gate at the rear.
As I stand at that front gate I hear,
an angelic choir from within those Golden Walls.
I walked around the rear, only to hear,
sad, wailing sounds and painful howls.
Quite shocked was I to hear my name called to a gate,
thank you, my God, for calling me to the Golden Gate.
It opened for my grand entrance into my new home,
Hallelujah, hallelujah, sang that lovely angelic choir,
then I joined in,
Never had I heard my voice sound like an angel,
the stunningly radiant faces of family and old friends,
now appeared into view,
I then saw a light so radiantly bright, it blinded me.
Here is the One I had prayed so hard I might see,
peace of God beyond all understanding,
just love and joy, but nothing demanding,
I have been invited in, to live here for eternity,
in the presence of the most Holy Trinity.
I shall always pray for you.
You, also, can imagine!
Amen, amen, amen.

# HEROES ALL

In my sleep last night I dreamed,
of our people who have died in wars,
at sea, in the air, and on foreign land,
then I heard the mournful sound,
of taps being played by an angel bugle band.

Then I listened to the cries and wails,
from all of those survivors I dreamed of,
those loved ones who've been left behind,
with so many memories of years gone by,
life now has become very cruel and unkind.

Those who made their ultimate sacrifice,
in so many wars, they have given their lives,
I then heard the celestial voice of God the Father,
Who said, "None of these people should have died,
on earth they're referred to as 'cannon fodder.'"

He continued speaking and went on to say,
"I have opened heaven's gates to allow them in,
they will spend eternity with me in My kingdom,
for all of the terrible sacrifices they all have made,
they battled and died for their nation's freedom."

I was then awakened from my dreaming,
I heard no further crying and screaming,
but I so vividly recall the details of my dream,
I now lay wondering why we have these wars,
begun by a horrible leader of a rogue regime.

# HEADSTONE ON AN EMPTY GRAVE

Uncle Mike was wounded in France,
where he served in World War I.
He came home, married my aunt Francis,
then on their farm, raised five tough sons.

Carl and Ray, the youngest two,
joined our nation's fight in World War II.
Very soon, Carl faced many great dangers,
he died in North Africa with the Army Rangers.

On the Atlantic, in a very short battle,
Ray, an armed guard on a merchant's vessel,
was sunk by a German U-boat torpedo,
to his family, that was another terrible blow.

Carl's body is buried with his mom and dad,
but there is something here so very sad,
Ray was lost at sea, his body never found.
Now there's a headstone on an empty grave,
in that same family plot of ground.

Let us not forget the POW and MIA,
always remember, for them we pray,
on this and every Memorial Day.
Give honor to all who have served in
so many terrible wars.
May they rest in eternal peace.
May all wars forever cease.

# HE IS WATCHING

It is a very troubled, unkind world,
that we are now living in,
so very many dreadful crimes,
and with every kind of sin.

We must hear and follow,
the Word of God,
that's the only solution
that I can see,
to make the world safe,
and sane again for everyone,
including you and me.

This is what I see
in my imagination:

In frustration and vexation,
with a huge tear in His eye,
God looks down from His throne,
up in heaven, on high,
He shouts out to all nations,

"People, people, people,
what have you done?
with my beautiful creation,
you have brought me
much frustration
and vexation,
you have polluted,
your water, land, and air,
there is death
and destruction everywhere.

Millions of infants' lives
have now been taken,
I love them dearly,
their lives have not been
forsaken,
their sinless souls
are here, with me,
in heaven, for eternity.

I find all this so very
repugnant,
I watch it all,
and shake my head,
just remember,
I'll sit in final judgment
someday,
when you're all dead.

I'll be leaving you now,
then I'll just wait and see,
after this stern reminder,
whether or not, you
have listened.

# HAVE YOU LOST YOUR WAY

Do you feel that your world is spinning out of control,
that you are rapidly falling into a huge dark hole?
Could it be that the principal reason for this is,
you have forgotten to have daily contact with Jesus?

When did you last get down on your knees and pray,
was it a year ago, month, week, yesterday, or today?
Did you ask Him to help you bear your heavy burden,
have you listened to a meaningful biblical sermon?

When was the last time you attended worship in the house of God,
did you feel completely at home there, or did it feel odd?
God has noted your long absence and sent you a call,
to hear the Gospels of Mathew, Mark,
Luke, John, and letters of Paul.

# HAPPY EASTER!

Lent brings forty days of Meditation,
Palm Sunday triumphant entry Celebration,
with the last week of Veneration,
Holy Thursday, Last Supper Consecration,
Good Friday, Day of Lamentation,
Holy Saturday, a Day of Preparation,
Easter Sunday, that Great Day of Jubilation.
"Why do you look for the living among the dead?
He is risen; He is not here,"
Luke's written affirmation.
Go, live in the peace of the risen Christ,
May He bless you all!
HAPPY EASTER!

# DOGGIE HEAVEN

I wonder if God made a doggie heaven,
which He created, then set aside,
for our loyal, faithful, furry friends,
who had been always at our side,
until they met their untimely ends.

In that special doggie heaven,
a place filled with doggie toys,
I wonder if there's a golden hydrant,
just for those doggie boys,
that would seem to be a requirement.

My German shepherd, RinTin,
and Mickey, my rat terrier,
would certainly have made the cut,
but not Buster, my English bulldog,
he was mean and just an awful mutt.

But who am I to judge their worth,
I lived with some of them for years,
when they still romped and played,
while they still lived upon this earth.
(I truly hope that Buster "made the grade.")

# Demons on This Earth

I think that hell must be totally empty,
for there are so many devils on earth.
They have done bad things aplenty,
our world needs a new rebirth.

They want to remove God's great plan,
create hatred, where Jesus preached love.
Jesus's words taught us to love our fellow man,
words from His Father in heaven above.

So as you go about your busy, daily life,
keep His words in your hearts and minds.
Hatred of another has caused much civil strife,
it has been with us since the dawn of mankind.

# Cheerful Charlie Downs

I observed a man today,
while walking in the mall,
he was just a bit rotund,
stood five and a half feet tall,
a cowboy hat adorned his head,
his caregiver walked on up ahead,
Charlie followed, waved to one and all,
and gave them a bright and happy smile,
only a few folks ignored his greeting,
but most of us, he did beguile,
we eagerly responded to his love,
I named him Cheerful Charlie Downs,
an angel sent down from above,
God's personal ambassador of goodwill,
to all he gave his peace and love,
for familial love, our need he did fulfill,
his wave seemed to be his personal blessing,
which he lovingly bestowed on everyone,
it seemed that God's love, he was expressing.
The parents of this lovable young man,
must feel great pride in their fine son.
Thank you, Cheerful Charlie Downs,
you have really made my day,
I trust that when I'm again in town,
you will again walk along my way.

# AUTUMNAL BEAUTY

So!
Autumn has again arrived!
The hot, humid days of summer are gone.
We stand now in awestruck wonder,
at nature's annual beauty pageant.
In the spectacular colors that surround us,
The Painter again displays His artistry,
by His masterful use of pallet and brush.

Stand quiet and still for a moment or two,
beneath the clear blue sky.
Take in those wonderful golds, yellows,
crimsons, greens, and browns, in hues,
that delight the most discerning eye.

Gaze across plain, hill, and valley,
then appreciate that, which God and nature,
have provided for your edification.
Those magnificent deciduous shade trees of summer,
have been transformed into a tapestry of color,
soon to disappear.
They will stand almost denuded,
except for those few hardy leaves,
which refuse to let go,
lest they be covered with the long winter's snow.

No, they will challenge the northerly winds of winter,
to remove them from their perch.
Watch them shiver in the breeze,
'til the warming sun of spring,
brings forth the transfusion of sap,
through the trees' arteries.

Then, once again, life returns,
to provide the shade for summer,
to our great delight.
Make plans now,
for your summer vacation.
Wear COVID masks, of course!

What a wondrous cycle!

# The Voice of an Angel

When I listened to this lady sing,
her voice would delight my ears,
I heard those mournful lyrics,
which filled my eyes with tears.

She sang about her lonely life,
and how she'd given up hope,
of ever becoming a loving wife,
now that she was hooked on dope.

It began when she turned seventeen,
she met this heroin pusher and user,
this doped-up dude was so very mean,
his biggest joy was to use her and abuse her.

This story about her wasted life is so very sad,
she had so much tender music in her voice,
what this pusher did to her makes me so darn mad.

We know that using drugs was not her choice,
but she will never sing again, on earth.
The angels will enjoy her angelic voice,
there she'll have a new rebirth.

So be it, amen.

# THE ADORATION CHAPEL

I sit alone in this holy place,
in total silence, with the Holy Spirit,
in this most serene Adoration Chapel,
restoring my soul and giving me peace of mind.
Alone? Not really, for I am in God's presence,
truly, a warm and loving peace do I find.

Kneeling here in silent, solemn prayer,
I'd rather spend an hour here, than anywhere.
I came here again today in prayer and meditation,
for my ultimate departure from my time on earth,
time spent here in silent adoration,
will be time well spent in preparation,
for my long life's inevitable cessation.

Please join me for one hour as Jesus asked,
"Do you not have one hour to spend with me?"
I pray your happiness will never cease.
May God love you,
and give you eternal peace!

# STREET LIVING

Drugs and booze, spousal abuse,
some gave up, saying what's the use.
Some have problems with mental health,
unemployed, they have no wealth.
Many now live in a battered tent,
they have no money to pay rent.
They shoot up dope with a syringe,
something that does make us cringe.
They live on the streets or in a park,
some dangerous places after dark,
or even during the light of day,
for many, death is not too far away.
From a gun, or knife, or fentanyl,
or in their stupor, they trip and fall.
A hundred thousand deaths in the USA,
that is a very costly price to pay.
Overdosing on heroin, cocaine, or opioids,
too many lives have been destroyed.
What is being done to stop this cycle,
for this kind of living is suicidal?
Now crack pipes are given to the addicts,
this cycle of addiction will go on, I'd predict.
But for the grace of God, there go I,
or you, or someone for whom we'd cry.

# No, It Can't Be Me

This morning, I looked into the looking glass,
and staring back at me,
were the tired eyes of some old man,
it was so sad to see.

I studied his face for a short while,
I could see from his intensive stare,
there was no one home,
there was just no one there.

His wrinkled face and thin gray hair,
made him look so very old,
I smiled at him, he smiled at me,
then he spoke solemnly.

His voice was one I'd heard before,
so I listened attentively,
he said, "You're looking old, my friend,"
and then he spoke some more.

I was once a young man,
that was so very long ago,
but looking back at those times,
there were things I did not know.

I didn't think I'd get this old so soon,
but I'm still here today,
when I walk from room to room,
I get lost along the way.

# MISGUIDED YOUTH

If you play around with drugs and carry a gun,
You're heading in the wrong direction, son.
You'd have a lot less stress and much safer life,
Not to mention the excess sorrow and strife.

First, you must discover who you really are,
Before you'll be doing a hard time behind prison bars.
Go talk to an ex-con who has now gone straight,
He'll tell you it's a hard and lonely life,
Behind those steel prison gates.

But the first thing you should do,
Have a serious talk with God, listen to His voice.
He probably will tell you,
Drugs and guns and a life of crime,
Are not a very wise choice.

In the end, my son, it's all up to you,
I cannot tell you what to do.
You can save yourself and change directions,
Or be a guest of the,
Minnesota Department of Corrections.

# Life Goes On

My life goes on, for better or worse,
'til I'm carried away in a big black hearse.
I have no control over most events,
some of those things just make no sense.

I love our nation, and I hope you do,
I'm a loyal American, through and through.
I salute the flag, when it's raised up high,
right hand on my heart, when it passes by.

I joined the navy, when just a young lad,
I've lived in good times, I have seen bad.
Now here I am in my last few years,
when the Lord calls me, I'll have no fears.

# HELP THE POOR

What do I want? What do I need?
Keep life simple, my friend.
There'll be much less worry,
when you reach your end.

What might I do,
for another today?
Show love and kindness,
that's all I can say.

Love your neighbor.
Give alms to the poor.
You must go find them.
They won't come to your door.

Shelter the homeless,
a bed and pillow,
for their weary head.
They feel such aloneness,
They need peace instead.

They could be you,
or someone you love,
but for the kindness,
of He, from above.

# Final Questions

What language is spoken in heaven?
What songs do the angels sing?
Are there churches, temples, or synagogues?
Do any have bells that ring?

We're told there is love and peace up there,
and God will greet each one who enters in.
There is an exclusive entry, we are aware,
the Holy Books say one must be without sin.

Please send us a message, when you arrive,
to let us all know what you have learned,
of parents, family, or friends, for we're still alive.
This was the destination for which they all yearned.

# SAUL'S ROAD

It was not a rapturous moment he spent,
with this person he met,
'twas on the road to Damascus, you see,
he heard his name called out,
he had no idea what this was all about.
"Saul, Saul, why do you persecute me?"
He asked, "Who is that speaking?"
"It is I, Jesus, whom you are persecuting."
Saul was blinded by a bright light,
which caused him to lose his sight.
"What is it that you want me to do?"
"Go into the city and there,
you will be told what to do."
Saul now blinded was led into the city,
he didn't eat for three days,
Jesus showed him much pity,
there, his sight was restored.
From then on, it was Christ he adored,
converted and baptized in Damascus,
by a Christian named Ananias.
A remarkable miracle, if you'd ask us.
After Paul's great conversion,
and baptism by immersion,
in Damascus, he preached,
"Jesus is truly the Son of God."
He preached wherever he went,
"To be saved, all sinners, must repent."
He preached the Gospel to the masses,
in so very many far-off places.
Known as "Apostle to the Gentiles"
his Jewish name Saul became Paul,
then people heard his own version,
of how he, through Jesus, came to conversion.
Although this entire episode seems odd,
Paul had been sent forth by God.

# O Lord, Transplant Our Hardened Hearts

O Lord, transplant our hardened hearts,
with hearts filled with peace, joy, and love,
please, let not our anger keep us far apart,
send down your healing love from above.

Please, Lord, transplant our hardened hearts,
with hearts filled with love, and joy, and peace,
take away the hatred that keeps us so far apart,
please stop the awful rioting, let this anger cease.

Today when I awoke, I heard your voice,
"Do not be filled with anger and hate,
toward this wonderful nation,
you live in freedom in the United States.
This land is the entire world's destination.
It is a shining beacon."

From many foreign lands, they come like ocean tide,
some with proper documentation, millions with none,
can be seen attempting to cross, they run and hide,
many are carrying illegal drugs, they enter, then run.

We're blessed to live in this greatest nation on earth,
even our currency proclaims, "In God, we trust,"
a phrase that should have been used since our nation's birth.
Let us pray for the survival of the USA, that's a must.
O Lord, transplant our hardened hearts.

Therefore, as the Holy Spirit says:

"Oh, that today you would hear His voice,
harden not your hearts."

# NOT ACCEPTABLE

We know there are many racists,
in every nation on this earth,
they come in every color and creed,
is this the result of low self-worth?

If you can only see yourself as a victim,
and blame others for your plight,
caused by those of different color,
perhaps you should be more contrite.

Let us look deeply within ourselves,
should we really lay blame on others,
our fathers abandoned us at birth,
to be raised by our single mothers.

———

"God knows
God knows there's a purpose,
God knows there's a chance,
God knows you can rise above
the darkest hour
Of any circumstance."
—Bob Dylan

———

The answer to these racist allegations,
is not in teaching critical race theory,
in our publicly funded schools,
many folks know this is Marxist teaching,
if we all accept CRT, we are fools.

# No More Abuse

You once told me that you loved me,
I now know that's not true.
You beat me, and you choke me,
I'm always black and blue.

I could go home to Dad and Mom,
I fear, for them, it's too much stress.
They'd be shocked to see what's going on,
to learn about my personal mess.

Eight weeks ago, you broke my wrist,
when you threw me up against the wall.
Today, you punched me with a clenched fist,
then you chased me down the hall.

You grabbed me and pulled me by the hair,
you threw me down on the floor.
After I got up, you choked me on a kitchen chair,
then you ran out, angry, and slammed the door.

The neighbors heard your curses and my wail,
then, thank God, they called 911.
Police arrived and took you to the county jail,
I've decided, now I'm going to run.

You called my cellphone demanding that I pay your bail,
I laughed out loud at your request.
"Think of how you've hurt me, and why you're in jail,
I fear you no more, for you have put me to the test."

There's a good man out there, somewhere,
now searching, for a loyal, loving wife.
In hope that he'll find me, I now say a prayer,
"God, give me a man who will love me all of my life."

I am living in transitional housing now,
I'm healing here, from those past sorrows.
I know God will work this out somehow,
I anticipate many happy, loving tomorrows.

I forgive you for what you have done to me,
since you might just be sick of mind.
I pray that someday you will clearly see,
that you can't go through life, being so unkind.

I pray to God that you will receive the mental help you need,
before you beat and make another loyal, loving woman bleed.

Peace be with you!

# Night Rain

A pounding, driving rain last night,
with the sound of rumbling thunder,
flashes and crashes of lightning strikes,
woke me rudely from a deep slumber.

I arose and looked out the bedroom window,
then watched those fireworks in the skies,
I wish I had recorded this amazing picture show,
quite an incredible spectacle, before my eyes.

I lay back down on my bed again,
then recited a prayer of thanks to the Lord,
for sending down to earth, badly needed rain,
our prayers for rain, He has not ignored.

When rain is needed on some future day,
God, we'll once again turn to You in prayer,
but right now, we are grateful, so we all say,
we'll also pray to You, when we're not in despair.

# Love Is Eternal

I have deep feelings of consternation,
regarding the situation in our nation,
so I spend much time in contemplation,
asking myself, What is the real causation?

Therefore, let us do an evaluation,
we might discover a revelation,
or we might end in desolation,
or perhaps in intense vexation.

Might it be our diverse population,
which requires difficult conflation,
how do we blend this cultural amalgamation,
for peace and tranquility in our great nation?

Let's all offer some humble propitiation,
lest this lead us all to possible damnation,
should we not learn to solve this situation,
let's give thanks and, together, have a celebration.

Through hard work and determination,
with never any cessation of endless motivation,
give thanks to the Lord for His great creation,
of these United States, a truly blessed nation.

We have been witnessing,
the emotional evisceration of our population.

# Live with His Love

In the morning, you see the rising sun,
witnessing a new life, that's just begun.
If today, you seek personal discipline,
then let your search begin within.

If it's happiness you wish to find,
start the search inside your mind.
Rid yourself of needless worry,
do nothing which will make you sorry.

Wear a friendly smile on your face,
look for the good in the human race.
Don't worry about things you cannot change,
daily events in our world are often strange.

When you approach the end of your life,
recall how you've handled sorrow and strife.
Many folks pray daily, asking God above,
to protect and guide them with His great love.

# LISTEN, MY CHILDREN

When your body is empty,
then heaven gains one,
it might be you, daughter,
or it might be you, son.

Remember, to go there,
you must live without sin,
that is the price of admission,
for you to enter in.

Too many people,
die unexpected,
the Bible tells us that,
someday, in the future,
we'll be resurrected.

So, children of God,
always live a clean life,
pray that He keep you,
from sin, sorrow, and strife.

On some day, yet unknown,
you'll be summoned to go,
to stand before God,
in your new heavenly home.

"While the body is empty,
I'm with you in spirit."
Amen!

# LET'S LOVE THE TREES

Here we are, raking leaves again,
always fighting against the wind,
it seems they are blown right back,
where they had originally been,
ultimately you get them into a stack,
then corral them into a big black sack.

They were so beautiful just days ago,
in colorful splendor while on the trees,
we look at empty branches now,
they have surrendered to a wild breeze.

Looking ahead to the coming spring,
which now seems so far away,
the sun will warm the trees and bring,
tiny buds, which will again be on display.

Last spring's buds I have not yet forgotten,
my itchy red eyes and constant sneezing,
because of tree pollen, I felt so rotten.
We have no pollen, when outside it's freezing.

At times, I sneeze with all my might,
my little dog is often filled with fright,
friends and family, take great delight,
with these words, "*Mein Herr gesundheit!*"

In their shade in summer, we grill and play,
the trees provide a protected place to nest,
for those songbirds, which awaken us each day,
this, my friends, is nature at its best.

# LET US PRAY

Prayer is a direct connection to the ear of God,
to the nonbelievers, this might seem quite odd,
but those beliefs and opinions are only theirs,
I'll continue, always, to say my prayers.

These are words that Jesus had spoken,
"Knock and the door shall be opened,
ask and you shall receive, seek and you shall find,"
He gave us many reasons we should all be kind.

So at the beginning and end of every day,
set aside some time to contemplate and pray,
pray for those who do not believe in Jesus,
if they all converted, it would surely please us.

So pray for me, and I'll pray for you,
Jesus has told us what we should do,
"Pray for one another that you may be healed,"
if we all did that, our faith would be revealed.

# Let Us Love Our Neighbor

Anger and resentment, let us set aside.
In our wonderful nation,
let us show our love and pride.
Please don't hate me for the color of my skin.
For God has blended many different pigments in.

United we will stand, strong and tall.
While divided, we will fail and fall.
Let us all thank our loving God,
and ask His forgiveness for our sin,
of hating folks with different colored skin.

# Afterward

There's a teardrop in the eye
of the old man in my coffin,
being shed for those I leave behind.
To my wife and family and my friends, I ask,
to each other please be kind.
You have just one life to live,
and so much love that you must give.
Share that love with all of humankind.
Christ instructed us to love our God,
and our neighbor, just as we love our self.
That is not so hard to do.
It is entirely up to you.

# Happy as a Bird

The robins sing early mornings in spring,
sitting high in a tree on their perch,
they sing praises to God for this beautiful day,
I think of them as singing in their church.

An oriole sings from the very top of a tree,
a spirited, melodic song for us,
soon to be joined by a sparrow, a cardinal,
and even a murder of crows,
all of them joining in the chorus.

Their songs remind me of the old hymns,
from the choir in church, where we always sing,
"Glory, Glory," "We Gather Together,"
and the uplifting,
"On Eagle's Wings."

What a wonderful way to begin our day,
those songs bring us such great pleasure,
just listening to those joyous sounds,
we all enjoy nature's melodic treasures.
"Be as happy as a bird today."

# A FRAIL OLD MAN

While walking through the park today,
I observed this frail and pale old man,
as he limped along leaning upon his cane,
his deeply wrinkled, weathered face,
showed that he walked in extreme pain.

He ambled over to a park bench,
I feared that he was about to faint,
he sat down with great effort,
and moaned without restraint,
I hurried over to assist as best I could,
I greeted him, but I don't think he understood.

On closer examination, I concluded,
that he was from some foreign land,
when he spoke he said, *"Buenos dias, senor,"*
I knew that he was a Latino gentleman,
In reply, said I, *"Como esta usted, mi amigo,"*
His response was, *"Malo, malo mucho."*

I told him to wait right here on a park bench,
while I run back to my house and bring my car,
then I will take him to the hospital ER,
when I returned it was quite apparent to me,
that he had fallen and injured his head,
this situation looked so very grim,
I rushed over to examine him,
it was quite apparent that he was dead.
*Lo siennto, lo siento, lo siento, mi amigo!*
*Descansa en paz!*

# Living on Borrowed Time, on Loan from God

I now find myself living,
in my twilight years,
many years beyond earlier expectations,
as I approach that final midnight hour,
I have no fears,
since I do believe in the teachings,
of Jesus Christ,
I fear no evil and shed no tears.
I look forward to the day when I shall meet Him,
with impassioned anticipation.
I believe in life eternal,
that life which Jesus promises to us,
"Believe in me, and you shall never die."
I love Him and accept as fact His words,
for He was never known to lie.
I know not the year, the month, the week,
the day, the hour, the minute, or the second,
nor where or how I'll be taken,
when God will call me home.
But I am convinced that should I go,
without sin on my soul,
I shall never, by Christ, be forsaken.
Each new day tells me that this life,
will not continue or forever go on,
that day approaches when I will be taken,
then from this earth, I shall be gone.
May God be loving and kind,
to those I leave behind.
So be it, amen

# PENSIVE THOUGHTS

Shh——
Be still.
Be still, be silent.
Turn off the world.
Relax your busy, worried mind,
if just for a moment or an hour.
Even better, give your soul peace,
for an entire day.
Appreciate what God has given,
for you to cherish and love,
often referred to as gifts from above.
Your family, your friends,
all of those upon whom you depend.
Be in awe of the sun on this beautiful day.
Those singing birds,
the wonderful children at play.
Show your love for all whom you meet.
Give a warm greeting to all people,
you might meet on the street.
Count all your blessings,
which God has provided,
for your use on earth.
Look around you at all of this,
for nothing do you own.
As has been said many times,
"From God, this all is just on loan."
Nothing but you is displayed,
at the funeral home.
May you rest in final peace.
Be still, be silent.
Be still.
Shh——

# ASHES TO ASHES, DUST TO DUST

This cross of ashes,
drawn upon the head,
the priest says the words,
"Remember thou are dust,
and unto dust, you shall return."
In our hearts, for heaven we yearn.
We wear them humbly this entire day,
in repentance for our sins, we must pray.
In biblical times, sackcloth worn on bare flesh,
they'd fall upon their knees and to God confess,
My Lord, my God, my sins have gravely offended thee.
Please, God, grant me pardon, from sin please set me free.
A good confession of our sins,
that's the way that Lent begins.
Fast, abstain, give alms to the poor,
don't turn them away from your door.
On Palm Sunday, He rode into Jerusalem,
on the back of a donkey, as palms were lain.
"Hosanna, the son of David. Hosanna in the highest,
blessed is He who comes in the name of the Lord."
The Last Supper, on Holy Thursday, our Holy Eucharist,
The abject torture of Jesus on Good Friday of Holy Week,
His scourging, the Crown of Thorns placed on Jesus's head.
He carried that heavy cross to Golgotha, He'd soon be dead.
His crucifixion on that cross—pierced in His side with that lance,
Then Jesus died such a cruel and ignominious death on that cross.
On the third day, they found the stone rolled back, an empty tomb!
He had risen from the dead and ascended
into heaven, with His Father.
He sacrificed His life for us, so we might have
eternal life in heaven with God.
He has risen, in all His glory!
Hosanna in the highest!
Happy Easter!

# YOU'RE SO LUCKY!

You might have wrinkled skin,
and brittle bones at ninety,
please don't feel that you're,
being treated too unkindly,
you complain of arthritic pain,
you're now walking with a cane,
thank God, you aren't walking blindly,
and you still have a clear-thinking brain.

If you woke up this morning,
and could rise up from your bed,
stop right now and thank the Lord,
that you are not yet dead,
you still can walk, even with that cane,
to get from here to there,
things, you know, could be much worse,
were you confined to a wheelchair.

Enjoy the remainder of your life,
in a thankful and positive frame of mind,
give thanks to God who watches over you,
that you are not in a home, confined,
appreciate each minute of each day,
you are still able to dress yourself,
you can bend and tie your shoes,
without the help of anyone else.

You have an active mind and body,
by the grace of God.

# Life and Love Are Gifts

A baby cries tears of happiness at birth,
thankful that it has been allowed to live,
nothing in this world compares to its worth,
girl or boy, they have so much love to give.

Thank you, my father and my mother,
for bringing me into this great world,
you are the very best, I want no other,
when you hold me, I hear you chuckle.

I know you'll always give me all your love,
and teach me to be a credit to you both,
praying for guidance from above,
watching my physical and spiritual growth.

Today, I look back on our many years of life,
when you helped me find my way each day,
I remember well the sorrow and strife,
I did not disappointment you too much, I pray.

As a postscript, I say to you,
Father and mother,
Husband and wife,
God bless you both,
For my life.

# You Are Blessed If You Have

A loving spouse or partner in your life,
a loving husband, with a happy family and wife,
a loving, loyal, trusted friend,
upon whom you always can depend.

A safe, warm place in which to reside,
with your loving family by your side,
without unnecessary sorrow or strife,
so you all might live a healthy, happy life.

Employment with adequate compensation,
enough to save for the needs of a coming day,
should you encounter a desperate situation,
and unforeseeable hard times come your way,

Good health of body and mind,
for you, your family, and your friends,
might you never be confined,
in a hospital, or long-term care.

Belief and faith in God's Son, Jesus,
Who will lead you to His home,
where you will live on in eternity,
when your days on earth are done.

# You Can't Go Home Again

I drove back to my old hometown,
In heavy, blinding rain,
the purpose of my trip was,
to see old friends again.

In the rain, I drove along,
Singing, "Glory, Glory," my own song,
suddenly, the rain just stopped,
my coming here felt so wrong.

I turned off the highway,
then continued on to the main,
I was really quite surprised,
since nothing looked the same.

I saw people on the sidewalks,
but there were none I knew,
I drove up and down the streets,
then said, "I know what I will do."

"I'll go out to the graveyard,
to see old familiar names."
I walked through the old iron gate,
this didn't look quite the same.

I checked the names on the tombstones,
and saw names I hadn't heard before,
so many foreign-sounding names,
this was just too hard to ignore.

I walked to the oldest burial sites,
ah, here were the names I knew,
the people I'd driven here to see,
I'll just name a few.

Eddie and Pigeon, Booby and Tom,
Fluky and Bobby, Harry and John,
Girls we all went to school with,
Patsy, Ding, Karen, and LaVon.
These, the old friends I came to see,
I found them here in this cemetery,
I hadn't known that they had died,
with much emotion, I stood and cried.

Many more names I read as I walked,
so many memories of the good times,
those weren't rich times, we were poor,
right then, I heard the church bells chime.

It was time to leave this hallowed ground,
I went back into town and drove around,
for one more look at what used to be,
way back then, this was home to me.

I drove up the street where I once lived,
it was something I had to do,
the old home was in shambles now,
it had been built back in 1902.

I walked up the broken sidewalk,
from the rotting porch, I peered inside,
broken windows and fallen plaster,
my sadness I couldn't hide, so I cried.

I left my old hometown that day,
I shall never return again,
I don't know what I can say,
I am feeling too much pain.
I shall not return again.
Amen.

# Who Is to Blame for a World Gone Insane?

Does the madness and sadness of our world,
cause God to tremble in anger,
or does He think to Himself, *What fools they are,
to have brought about so much danger,
to themselves and all future generations?*

He created us and loves us all,
after all, He sent His beloved Son to teach us,
to love one another, just as He loves us,
to be patient and kind,
to turn the other cheek when injured by another,
to honor and respect your father and your mother,
please save sweet, innocent babies,
who their lives must give, but if allowed to live,
might become those who show us all the way,
for them, we all must pray.

Christ loved those innocent children,
"Let those innocent children come unto me,
if you harm these innocent children,
it is better that a millstone be tied around your neck,
and you be drowned in the depths of the sea."
All of these babies have been forsaken.
Let us lament the more than sixty million,
who have been so brutally taken.

# THOUGHT-PROVOKING INTERLUDE

While on my morning walk on a sunny day,
I stepped inside Saint Joseph Church to pray.
The sun shone on those beautiful stained-glass prisms,
my mind then thought about the holy oil of chrism,
which the priest applies to the chest and head,
of a baby, receiving the sacrament of baptism,
upon the forehead of a confirmand at confirmation,
anointing of the hands of a priest at ordination,
upon the forehead of a new bishop,
by the consecrating bishop.

*Oleum infirmorum* (oil of the sick),
anoints the head,
of the gravely ill and dying,
those who are almost dead.
The priest recites the prayers of Extreme Unction,
at this hour of life and death's junction.

It brings the grace of God to this troubled soul,
whose greatest hope in life has been,
to live with God that heavenly goal.
I'm here today in God's house,
to confess my sins,
praying to Him that when I die,
He will open heaven's doors,
and allow me in.
Amen.

# The End Shall Come One Day

I'm never alone, with you in my heart,
You're there to show me the way,
to that eternal place of happiness, I seek,
to reach that goal, I pray each day.

I pray that You'll take my hand, dear Jesus,
and lead me to that home of final peace,
with all of the saved who have gone on before,
where those heavenly joys never cease.

The end shall come, when least expected,
I am well protected by You, my Lord,
Your teachings, I have always accepted,
It is You, I have always adored.

# Queen Elizabeth, in Memoriam

Elizabeth, Queen of the Commonwealth,
passed away on September 8, in poor health,
for seventy years she was loved so much,
Queen Elizabeth had that motherly touch.

She passed away on September 8, 2022,
she was very ill, nothing could her doctors do,
she lived a long, adventurous life of ninety-six years,
all over the world today, folks are shedding tears.

Her funeral at Westminster Abbey in ten days,
on September 19, burial at Windsor Castle.
Prince Phillip will be moved to be at her side,
with him, she ruled her kingdom with great pride

Rest in eternal peace, oh, gracious Queen,
you have never in your life done anything mean.
You're now in heaven with God the Father,
you were God's most loyal loving daughter.

RIP, Your Royal Highness!

# Love Your Unknown Neighbor

You are walking along,
on a cold city street,
would you buy food,
for a down-and-out stranger,
whom you should happen to meet?

Would you find shelter,
from the cold winter night,
a safe, warm bed,
a pillow for that tired, weary head,
a mansion, with toilet,
up just one flight?

No smoking or drinking,
does this place allow,
a place to relax,
protected from any violent acts,
tonight will be warmer
than sleeping out in the snow.

There, but for the grace of God,
might that be me,
if my fortunes had turned,
had all my bridges been burned,
a most horrible world,
would this world be.

# HOME OF FINAL PEACE

At the northwest edge of town, on a small hill,
a serene setting with much tranquil charm,
stands an authentic farm relic, an old windmill,
this is the homestead of the old Chladek farm.

In this grove of beautiful shrubs and trees,
sits a special residence, the homestead hospice,
where angels of mercy work so hard to please,
with loving care, those who will soon be at peace.

They love to care for those who will soon be gone,
as well as for those who linger on and on,
relatives, friends, and volunteers console the ill ones,
a chaplain prays with them, she is Sister Franchon.

This angel of God has worked tirelessly for many years,
witnessing countless sad endings, so many deaths,
with those grieving for their loved ones, having shed many tears.
in rooms of those heeding God's call, with their last breath.

One who, years ago, helped conceive of this wonderful home,
developed cancer while living out west in another state,
while suffering through this losing battle, he was never alone,
in this place where he returned to face his inevitable fate.

We have come here to console and grieve,
the loss of many good friends in previous days and years,
we were extremely saddened to see them all leave,
families, friends, and the angels of mercy all shed tears.

Please come and volunteer your time and talent,
caring for those who await that final call,
a memorial gift would be wonderful, indeed,
to defray the cost for those who have great need.
Thank you and God bless you.

# He Teaches Love and Truth

Please, God, transplant my hardened heart,
with a heart that's filled with holy love,
for Jesus Christ our Lord, Your only Son,
whom You sent down from above.

He came to redeem us from all our sins,
His teachings, we must all believe,
He was born to Mary in Bethlehem,
His crib a manger, on the first Christmas Eve.

Jesus's humble birth in a Bethlehem stable,
on that Christmas Eve, to His mother, Mary,
conceived by the power of the Holy Spirit,
she was chosen by God, His child to carry.

God the Father said, "Listen to Him,
I am the Way, the Truth, and the Life,
No one comes to the Father, but by Me,
Love one another as I have loved you,"
His teachings lead us to a happy afterlife.

# DREAM OF SUCCESS

"I am poor if I have no dream."
What do those words really mean?
I can recall my days of childhood,
much more than any child should.

I then had such a wild imagination,
especially during my summer vacation.
I'd lay on my back, looking up to the sky,
piloting a plane, which I'd learned to fly.

I built and flew my homemade kite,
on a string so long, it was almost out of sight.
Someday, I'm going to build a plane,
I'll fly that big bird in sunshine or rain.

Alas, those childhood ideas didn't evolve,
to build and fly a plane takes great resolve.
It also takes money and special knowledge,
special training, and five years of college.

I have now successfully fulfilled my dream,
as an adult, I know well what that means.
It took much work and determination,
fortitude, special training, and education.

My childhood dreams have now come true,
I fervently wish that all of yours have too.
That you, in your career, have great success,
which has resulted in your total happiness.

# THOUGHTS OF YOU

To my loving wife and family,
and to all of my good friends,
I speak to you quite candidly,
my love and respect, to you, I send.

In the morning, I awaken from my rest,
this is the way I start the day,
prior to my getting dressed,
I pause, then for each of you, I pray.

I thank God for your love and loyalty,
that He grant you a long and healthy life,
that you live your life quite joyfully,
without the burdens of sorrow and strife.

That you never lack life's necessities,
that you enjoy prosperity and wealth,
that you can handle life's complexities,
that He keep you safe and in good health.

My prayers are all-encompassing,
I do not use these words or phrases,
but I do ask for the good Lord's blessings,
upon each of you, for all your remaining days.

# THE TREE

I drove past this old lone tree,
It brought many memories back to me.
On the farm where this tree lives,
I spent summers with my relatives.

This tree stands out in a hay meadow,
I'd rake the hay my uncle had mowed.
I remember these apples were so sweet,
We'd walk over and pick a couple to eat.

We'd sit down in its shade to rest a while,
My uncle Jim could always get me to smile.
He told funny stories of when he was a kid,
The things he and his two brothers did.

Uncle Jim, how did this tree start to grow?
He told me his dad planted it fifty years ago.
He bought an apple at the country store,
He was making hay, then tossed the core.

Now seventy years old, it has grown so tall,
Producing sweet red apples every fall.
I walked up to pick some apples today,
Returned to my car, then went on my way.

I miss my uncle Jim and sweet Aunt Beth,
It has been twenty years since their deaths.
I have memories of my summers out here,
When I think of those days, I shed a tear.

From this tree, I can see the tall church steeple,
My aunt and uncle were church-going people.
For eternity, they live with Jesus in heaven,
That's what they always prayed for, amen.

# THE HATRED OF OUR TIMES

"Anyone who says I love God,
but hates his brother, is a liar."
(John 4:20)

There is too much hatred in this nation.
Is it brought about by miscommunication,
or perhaps, by cultural discrimination?

When we hate people of a different race,
rioting, burning, shootings are so commonplace.
Do we not understand that's a terrible disgrace?

Why do so many young folks die by drugs and guns?
We are losing too many of our daughters and sons,
that sad fact should be a concern for everyone.

It seems there is a correlation between this hatred,
and why the teachings of Jesus are so denigrated.
Let us recall the reason why we were created.

# MISLED YOUTH

We're witnessing such anxiety, consternation, and desperation,
in the minds of the pampered youth of our once great nation,
on the streets, they show faces of panic, anger, and hallucination,
and think they can overthrow the freedoms,
written in our "Independence Declaration."
They know little of our nation's history because of their
inadequate education,
Scholars say, "If we don't know our history,
We won't know our destination."

# Tale of Meeting a New Friend

I was walking down the street today,
considering things that I might say,
to the next person, whom I would meet,
when up beside me walked this old,
limping, sad-eyed, brown, shaggy-haired dog,
with large drooping ears and big wide feet.

I looked down at him, and he looked up at me.
"Good morning, dog," said I, then noticed,
that spirit of friendliness in his sad old eyes.
"How are things going for you, my friend?"
He, with a quiet bark, ruff, said he, ruff.
I agreed times are tough, really rough.

You look tired and hungry, and I am too,
so let's rest here in the shade for a minute or two.
I have a little treat for us to eat,
some cookies I brought, it was good planning, I thought.
I'd be happy to share with you this special treat.
I have some water too. I'll also share with you.

Let's talk for a while, "Where you from old pal?
Do you have a loving home, or just passing through,
our fair town, or perhaps just sniffing around for a new gal?"
In either case, I'm happy we have met.
I'd like to take you home with me, I know you'd be a wonderful pet.
Trouble is, I live a loner's life just as you do.
I do have a room in that nursing home where we just met.
On some future day, I will move again, I know not when nor where,
but I do hope that you'd come visit me once in a while.
Perhaps they do, but I don't know,
whether they'll allow old dogs there.
You might tell me why you've walked for so many miles.
We'll meet in some heavenly place where again we'll sit and talk,
about life and how it was a wonderful long walk.
That thought makes me smile.

# PRAY FOR THE USA

There is constant partisan bickering,
the people's work does not get done,
too much gridlock and petty fighting,
which harms the nation, in the long run.

It never ends, they spend and spend,
but never read the bills they pass,
someday, this will come to a bitter end,
repayment will befall the middle class.

Term limits you say, they just laugh at that,
they want to be the ruling class forever,
neither Republican, Socialist, nor Democrat,
all of them together, they're so very clever.

These folks dictate to us what we must do,
they make the laws that we must obey,
file our taxes or face Internal Revenue,
their laws are more oppressive every day.

There is no place on God's green earth,
where I would rather live and die,
yet, in the USA are many who yell and curse,
whom those politicians cannot satisfy.

"How to tell if some politicians are lying—
Their lips are moving."

# Observations of Nature

I am hiking along this paved walkway,
on this beautiful early autumn day.
The sun shines warmly down on me,
maybe there's something new I'll see.

I'll walk along for a mile or two,
observing what the wildlife do.
Squirrels gathering their winter supply,
geese flying high in the clear blue sky.

A bald eagle soaring high above,
searching for a tasty morsel to love.
The crows, as usual, foraging about,
they'll be successful, do not doubt.

A pair of mallards in the stream,
in season, they'd be a hunter's dream.
In the clear water, I see rainbow trout,
with my fly line, I could take them out.

Three does standing on a little hill,
a deer hunter could surely make a kill.
There runs a tasty bunny rabbit,
I saw that eagle swoop down and grab it.

I thank God for these magnificent creatures,
nature can be an excellent teacher.
Take time to observe wildlife near you,
I'm certain you'll learn something new.

# In God We Trust, or We Die

We've been dying since the day we were born,
for there are many who wish our demise.
Now more than ever before,
are we in danger
of losing the will
as a free nation to survive?
We were born into a life of freedom
in this great nation,
guided by the hand of God.
The Founding Fathers wrote
a fine proclamation:
The Declaration of Independence,
The Bill of Rights,
The Constitution,
and don't forget
*The Federalist Papers.*
But can all of this survive
the distortions and lies
of our politicians,
whose principal goal
is their reelection
and egocentric control
of WE, the people?
We, who have lived long lives,
have seen a different nation,
not at all like our current situation.
In politics, no longer is there civil discourse.
We are seeing the worst
while praying for the best, of course,
to save the United States
for future generations.
Prevail, we must.
The alternative
is deadly
for our nation.
God bless and preserve America!

# He Loves Us All—Shouldn't We Do Likewise?

God above still loves you,
even if you're filled with hate,
but when you hate another,
you might be lacking faith.

If Jesus stood before you,
could you look Him in the eye,
and tell Him that you love Him,
or just hang your head and cry?

Could you kneel and look up at Him,
and beg forgiveness for your sins,
including your hatred for others,
those of different color skins?

Please don't hate me if you see me,
if you meet me on the street,
since we don't know each other,
smile and wave, a great way to greet.

Let's make a firm commitment,
starting now, without delay,
let's change our hate-filled attitude,
ever onward, from this day.

If you believe Christ's teachings
He called us sisters and brothers,
this world would be so peaceful,
if we showed love for all others.

If you believe Christ's teachings,
I sincerely hope you do,
we must love God and our neighbor,
then peace will come unto you.

# CHRISTMAS BLESSINGS

The gifts are wrapped, beneath the tree,
the children ask, "Which one's for me?"
The cards are written and have been sent,
now we are awaiting that great event.

The birth of Christ on that Christmas Eve,
the greatest gift that we'll ever receive.
For had the Christ child never been born,
there would not be a Christmas morn.

Things would be different upon this earth,
since there would not be any Christian church.
We wouldn't have had the Immaculate Conception,
Christ's death upon the cross, nor His Resurrection.

Let us celebrate Christ's humble birth today,
let us all bow our heads and devoutly pray.
Thanks be to God the Father, in heaven above,
for giving us Jesus, who gives us His love.

A blessed Christmas, a sincere wish to all,
let us always respond to Christ's loving call.
Please attend a Christmas service in your church,
offer your prayers of thanks for Jesus's birth.

# Beauty, Painted by God

It's September 7, fall is near,
the nights are cool, the sky is clear.
Today, the temperature is 70 degrees,
colors are changing on the maple trees.

This trend will continue for several weeks,
then all the colors will be at their peaks.
What a beautiful sight for us to behold,
crimson, yellow, brown, tan, and gold.

I always think of this as God's masterpiece,
this beauty, framed, used as His mantelpiece.
Soon the wind will blow those leaves down,
they will be scattered all over the ground.

There soon will come two feet of snow,
no leaves to rake, no lawns to mow.
Start the snow blower and get shovels out,
that is what our winter is all about.

# AN OLD MEMORY

I struggled to climb a high mountain,
which looked out over that vast sea,
I stood there inhaling the ocean breeze,
memories of that terrible war, so long ago,
came flooding back to me.

A lad of just seventeen years, was I,
back in nineteen forty-four,
I wanted to join the United States Navy,
I convinced my mother to sign for me,
so I could go fight in that war.

I stand here on this high mountain today,
gazing out over that rough sea,
recalling those days of so long ago,
I'm now at the old age of ninety-four,
I will go sailing no more.

As I stand here today, recalling the past,
the things that I've seen and have done,
all of the friendships I made on my ship,
then, returning home was my final trip,
that long war had finally been won.

# A Boy's Best Friend

When I was just a young lad,
there was one friend I had,
he was loving and loyal to me,
we played out together,
no matter the weather,
me and my terrier, Mickey,
a dog, a great joy,
for every young boy,
they're always willing to play,
they'll chase a ball,
then return when you call,
and continue to do that all day.

When the school bus would stop,
and out I would hop,
he was happy to see me again,
if he could talk, he'd probably say,
"Where have you been, my good friend?
It's too long that you've been away."
When I went off to war,
he'd wait at the door,
hoping to see me walk in,
he felt so alone,
waiting for me to come home,
but I'd never see him again.

When I returned from the war,
and walked through the door,
my friend wasn't waiting to play,
then I learned he had died,
so I sat down and cried,
I shall never forget that day.
Mother put my slipper on his bed,

he'd lay on that slipper with his head,
he felt my presence that way,
he would carry it to the front door,
lay his head upon it on the floor,
maybe I'd be returning today.

# Kindness Rules

When I rise to greet another day,
After I have taken time to pray,
Let this thought be on my mind,
"To all others, I'll be kind."

"I'll bring happiness to those I can,
To every child, woman, and man,
Only kind words will I dare to speak,
No popularity do I seek."

"I'll greet everyone in a friendly way,
As I go about my affairs on this day,
It will become a habit, after a while
I shall make that my new style,"

Then at the end of this fine day,
I'll thank the Lord when I pray,
That now others will do the same,
If they don't, it will be a shame.

# MY LORD—

Let me live my life doing good works of mercy,
Deliver me from needless anxiety and worry,
There are so many things I can do for others,
Go visit the sick and lonely one who suffers,
Those who have no family or friends nearby,
I have seen them sit in their room and cry,
When a kind stranger comes into their room,
It is like a ray of sunshine, it lifts their gloom.
We learn of sad things they've lived through,
They'll explain to you why they just withdrew,
Veterans who experienced the ravages of war,
Or some folks who tell you they grew up poor,
Others who have had a happy and fulfilling life,
But we're devastated by losing a husband or wife,
You explain that there is hope even in darkness,
At times we encounter people who are heartless,
But we all know that our lives will someday end,
For most folks that's not difficult to comprehend,
My dear friend, let us now pray to God together,
That He accepts us into heaven, where all is better.
Amen.

# Love, Not Hate

There is too much hatred in our world today,
Please tell me, Jesus, has it always been this way,
Why can't we all live in peace, together,
Is it because some think they are so much better,
Or is it because they don't like the way we look,
About this subject, there are so many books.
But the one book upon which I depend,
One which theologians highly recommend,
is the Holy Bible, which lays out the rules,
if followed, will prevent our living like fools,
those guideposts, to a happy life and death,
might lead you to heaven, after your last breath.

# YOU CHOOSE

God above still loves you,
although you're filled with hate,
but when you hate another,
you might be lacking faith.

If Jesus stood before you,
could you look Him in the eye,
and tell Him that you love Him,
or hang your head and cry.

Could you look up to Him,
and beg forgiveness for your sin,
of hating all the others,
who have different color skin?

# WE'D MISS CHRISTMAS!

What if there had been no first Christmas?
I pondered that question today.
If Jesus Christ had not been born,
to whom would we Christians pray?

Who would have given us teachings,
about how to live and be happy in life?
About loving God and your neighbor,
without sinful pride, sorrow, and strife.

There would be no Christianity,
as we are known, as followers of Christ.
The world filled with even more insanity,
criminals would be more enticed.

There would be no churches anywhere.
Sunday would be just another day.
Christ would not have been born to Mary,
then laid in a manger filled with hay.

He wouldn't have been in the temple,
at the youthful age of twelve.
He would not have gone out to preach and teach,
then sacrifice his life for sinners, like myself.

Who would have selected twelve brave men,
to go forth and preach the gospel far and wide?
Who would have healed the sick and raised the dead?
Who would have been crucified on the cross and died?

There would have been no resurrection,
from the tomb hewn into the stone.
On the third day, no ascension,
without my Savior Jesus, I'd feel so all alone.

Jesus would not have died for you and me.
For our sins, there would be no redemption.
We could never live with Him in eternity.
This is all beyond my comprehension.

# ADDICTED NO MORE

Thank God for all those poor souls,
who have recovered from addiction,
it is so debilitating to go through life,
burdened by that dreadful affliction.

The poor addict and those loved ones,
husbands, wives, best friends as well,
have tried and cried and suffered too,
they've been put through a living hell.

We prayed someday they'd see the light,
their addicted minds will clear,
live clean for just one hour at a time,
then a day, week, month, and year.

The former addict looks back with pride,
on the years they've now been clean,
freed from the addiction they once tried to hide.
they say it was much easier than it seemed.

They thank God for their newfound serenity,
with the courage to change the things they can,
they are well pleased with their new identity,
and newfound wisdom, it's all in God's plan.

Jason Lennox has written a book,
which should be read by everyone,
booze and drugs got him hooked,
when he was so very young.

His book about addicted life,
is a book that should be read,
to learn of all the sorrow and strife,
we all thank God, he is not dead.

# HOLY MOMENT

Have you had a holy moment?
What do those words mean to you?
Let us all become proponents,
of doing what God wants us to do.

Holy moments make us better humans,
let us do the things that God expects,
I've come to the prudent conclusion,
that our actions have profound effects.

Helping a sick or needy neighbor,
do their shopping or mow their lawn,
doing so gives you a holy moment,
in that holy moment, you cannot go wrong.

Each day, we are asked to make decisions,
can we offer a holy moment now,
no matter what your religion is,
find time to do God's work somehow.

How many holy moments have you had,
that you now can call to mind,
where the results made you feel very glad,
you have shown you are loving and kind.

# LET US GIVE THANKS

Happy Thanksgiving to all of you.
We hope you enjoy this special day.
Spend time with friends and family,
please, do not forget to pray.

Offer thanks to our Almighty God,
for the food served at your table.
You've donated to feed the poor,
if financially, you were able.

102 Pilgrims on the *Mayflower* ship,
left England on a dangerous trip.
They sailed to a place they'd never been,
with no idea of what might happen to them.

On December 21, 1620,
they landed at Plymouth Rock,
the tiny ship had to anchor out,
since there was no dock.

King James the First of England,
persecuted these Christian Pilgrims,
that's why they sailed to this new land,
for freedom to practice their religion.

The Wampanoag tribe of Native Americans,
showed them how they can survive,
how to grow corn and how to hunt,
but at the end of that first winter,
only one half remained alive.

In November 1621, after a bountiful harvest of corn,
Governor William Braddock proclaimed a day of Thanksgiving,
"To render thanksgiving to Almighty God for all His blessings."
In 1623, he proclaimed Thursday, November 29,
as the official day for Thanksgiving.
In 1941, President Roosevelt and the Congress,
set Thanksgiving as the last Thursday of November.

# Seek Peace of Mind

Do you feel that your world is spinning out of control,
that you are rapidly descending into a huge dark hole,
could it be that the principal reason for all this is,
you have forgotten to have daily contact with Jesus.

When did you last get down on your knees and pray,
was it a year ago, month, week, yesterday, or today,
did you ask Him to help you bear your heavy burden,
when have you listened to a meaningful biblical sermon.

When did you last worship in the house of God,
did you feel at home there, or did it feel rather odd,
God has noted your long absence and sent you a call,
to hear the Gospels of the four evangelists and letters of Saint Paul.

Pray that you regain the tranquility you once enjoyed,
prior to the world's terrible events made you so annoyed,
pray fervently to the Lord for the forgiveness of your sins,
pray to Him for peace of mind, for there, happiness begins.

# ABOUT THE AUTHOR

Bud Peka was born on a farm near Crosby, North Dakota, in 1926. The Great Depression impoverished his family for years. At the age of seventeen, he joined the navy in WWII and saw action in the Pacific theater. He wrote his first poem for Mother's Day when he was seven years old and then continued to write when inspired. Bud has written over five hundred poems and many songs.

One song "Glory, Glory, Glory, How I Found the Lord" is copyrighted. It is played on several radio stations. It has been recorded by a bluegrass band in Tennessee, Blue Highway. The original version is available on YouTube, "Bud Peka KOWZ FM." Please listen to it and like it if you wish. Bud will continue to write as long as God inspires him and gives him the mental acuity to write.

Bud's poems are being printed weekly in area newspapers. He has had two books of poems published for local distribution and gifts. He sincerely hopes that you will enjoy this latest poetic endeavor. If so, please recommend it to others or give it to someone who might also enjoy it.

*****

It has been an honor for me to submit this work to all of you, readers. I thank you profusely. May God bless you with good health and happiness. God bless America.

—Bud Peka